THE WISDOM OF HILDEGARD OF BINGEN

THE
WISDOM
OF
HILDEGARD
OF
BINGEN

Compiled and introduced by

Fiona Bowie

William B. Eerdmans Publishing Company
Grand Rapids, Michigan

This edition published 1997 in the USA
through special arrangement with
Lion Publishing by
Wm. B. Eerdmans Publishing Co.
255 Jefferson Ave. S.E., Grand Rapids,
Michigan 49503

Printed in Singapore

01 00 99 98 97   7 6 5 4 3 2 1

ISBN 0-8028-3851-0

Series editor: Philip Law

Project editor: Angela Handley

Book designer: Nicholas Rous

Jacket designer: Gerald Rogers

CONTENTS

INTRODUCTION

Hildegard of Bingen is one of the best known religious figures of the Middle Ages. Her current reputation, after years of comparative neglect, is justly founded upon her visionary writings, her music and her role as a spiritual counsellor to many of the leading religious and political figures of her day.

Hildegard was born in Bermersheim in Rheinhessen in 1098, the tenth child of a noble family. From her earliest years Hildegard felt herself to be different from other people. She had strange visions (possibly related to migraines) and the ability to foresee everyday future events. At the age of eight Hildegard became the companion and pupil of a hermit, Jutta von Sponheim, who lived the enclosed life of a Benedictine anchoress attached to the nearby Benedictine monastery of Disibodenberg.

The enclosed religious life was not without its attractions for young women of noble birth and Jutta and Hildegard were soon joined by others. At the age of fifteen Hildegard took the habit of a Benedictine nun, and when Jutta died in 1136 she was elected as the leader (*magistra*) of the women's community. An important figure in Hildegard's life was the monk, Volmar, in whom she confided, and to whom she dictated what she had seen and heard from the Living Light. Volmar was convinced that Hildegard was divinely inspired rather than deluded, and acted as her scribe until his death in 1173. As Hildegard's reputation as a visionary and healer grew she began to correspond with many of the people who sought her help and advice, including kings and queens, abbots and abbesses, monks, nuns and lay people.

Around 1150 Hildegard left Disibodenberg to found a new community at Rupertsberg near Bingen, in the green, wooded Rhine valley. A daughter house at Eibingen, on the opposite bank of the Rhine, followed in 1165. Despite frequent ill health Hildegard continued to write both theology and music, as well as works of medicine and natural science, to undertake preaching tours and to lead her two communities. By the time of her death in 1179 Hildegard was one of the best known women in Germany, and soon became venerated as a local saint.

Hildegard's theology, which reflected the current hierarchical understandings of both the natural and supernatural order, was ambitious in scope, encompassing the whole of creation and of the history of God's dealings with humanity. Human beings are sinners in need of God's mercy, but created good, as is all of nature. God is life-affirming rather than life-denying, and virgins consecrated to the religious life are the jewel of this glorious creation. Greenness (*viriditas*) is one of Hildegard's favourite motifs, referring to the fruitfulness of the spiritual life as well as the health of the physical world. While it would be anachronistic to regard Hildegard as an ecologist or feminist, her firm grasp of the interconnectedness of all things and of the loving mercy of God, who fashioned the whole of creation out of love, continues to speak powerfully to us today.

FIONA BOWIE

THE WORK OF GOD

I

THE LIVING LIGHT GIVES HILDEGARD HER COMMISSION

 O poor little figure of a woman; you, who are the daughter of many troubles, plagued by a grave multitude of bodily infirmities, yet steeped, nonetheless, in the vastness of God's mysteries – commit to permanent record for the benefit of humanity what you see with your inner eyes and perceive with the inner ears of your soul so that, through these things, people may come to know their Creator and not recoil from worshipping God with due reverence. And so, write these things, not according to your heart but according to my witness – for I am Life without beginning or end.

De Operatione Dei, Foreword

THE CREATIVE SOURCE OF ALL BEING

I, the highest and fiery power, have kindled
every living spark and I have breathed out
nothing that can die. But I determine how
things are — I have regulated the circuit of the
heavens by flying around its revolving track
with my upper wings — that is to say, with
Wisdom. But I am also the fiery life of the
divine essence — I flame above the beauty of
the fields; I shine in the waters; in the sun, the
moon and the stars, I burn. And by means of
the airy wind, I stir everything into quickness
with a certain invisible life which sustains all.
For the air lives in its green power and its
blossoming; the waters flow as if they were
alive. Even the sun is alive in its own light;
and when the moon is on the point of
disappearing, it is kindled by the sun, so
that it lives, as it were, afresh.

De Operatione Dei, Vision One

THE WHEEL OF LIFE

The firmament has a revolving orbit in imitation of the power of God which has neither beginning nor end – just as no one can see where the encircling wheel begins or ends. For the throne of God is God's eternity in which God alone sits, and all the living sparks are rays of God's splendour, just as the rays of the sun proceed from the sun itself. And how could God be known to be life, except through the living things which glorify God, since the creatures which praise God's glory have come from God.

De Operatione Dei, Vision Four

THE RADIANCE OF CREATION

There is nothing in creation which does not have some radiance, either greenness or seeds or flowers or beauty — otherwise it would not be part of creation.

De Operatione Dei, Vision Four

THE WORK OF THE SOUL

Now the soul is a sensible spirit. It dwells in the heart where its wisdom is at home, and with this wisdom thinks through and arranges everything, just as the father of a family keeps his own affairs in order.

De Operatione Dei, Vision Four

THE HOLY SPIRIT
STRENGTHENS THE SOUL

The soul is strengthened to all manner of good
works by the fire of the Holy Spirit, but it is
weakened by the cold of indifference and
neglect. The powerful fire and its contrite
disposition mingle in human beings and bring
forth good fruit. If humans are overburdened
and wearied by sins, these sins will all gather
together, just as a fire is smothered by thick
smoke and can no longer burn brightly. But if
through the power of the soul the greed of
human desire is broken, then we burst out with
longing for the Father's heavenly home, just as
the bee constructs its comb from its own honey.
In this way the new works and old deeds of
human beings are so intermingled that they are
bound together in true humility, and the fire of
pride cannot consume or dry them up.

De Operatione Dei, Vision Four

THE ETERNAL WORD

The Word is light that has never been
concealed by shadow, never given a time to
serve or to rule, to wax or to wane. It is,
rather, the principle of all order and the Light
of all lights, which contains in itself light.
For God has never risen with the dawn nor
climbed with the morning sun. God has always
existed in eternity.

De Operatione Dei, Vision Four

KNOW THE WAYS
OF THE LORD

LOVE, HUMILITY AND PEACE

Everything that God has effected has been perfected in Love, Humility and Peace. Human beings, therefore, should esteem Love, embrace Humility and grasp Peace.

De Operatione Dei, Vision Eight

THE WILL

For the will is like a fire, baking each deed as if in a furnace. Bread is baked so that people may be nourished by it and be able to live. So too the will is the strength of the whole work, for it starts by kneading it and when it is firm adds the yeast and pounds it severely; and, thus preparing the work in contemplation as if it were bread, it bakes it to perfection by the full action of its ardour, and so makes a greater food for humans in the work they do than in the bread they eat. A person stops eating from time to time, but the work of the will goes on until the soul leaves the body. And in whatever differing circumstances the work is performed, whether in infancy, youth, adulthood or bent old age, it always progresses in the will and in the will comes to perfection.

Scivias, Book One, Vision Four

THE SOUL

Understanding in the soul is like the green
vigour of the branches and the leaves of a tree.
Will is like the flowers on the tree; mind like
the first fruit bursting forth. But reason is like
the fruit in the fullness of maturity; while
sense is like the height and spread of the tree.

Scivias, Book One, Vision Four

THE SACRAMENTS

I the Father am present to every creature and withdraw Myself from none; but you, a human being, withdraw from creatures. You look into water, and your face appears in it, but your reflection can exercise none of your powers, and when you turn away you no longer appear in the water. But I do not appear to creatures thus changeably; I am present to them in a true manifestation, never withdrawing My power from them but doing in them by the strength of My will whatever I please. And so too I truly display My majesty in the sacrament of the body and blood of My Son, and wondrously perform My miracles there from the beginning of the priest's secret words until the time when that mystery is received by the people.

Scivias, Book Two, Vision Six

TRUE WISDOM

You have been given great intelligence; and so great wisdom is required of you. Much has been given to you, and much will be required of you. But in all these things I am your head and helper. For when Heaven has touched you, if you call on Me I will answer you. If you knock at the door, I will open to you. You are given a spirit of profound knowledge, and so have in yourself all that you need.

Scivias, Book Three, Vision Ten

PURITY OF HEART

Many seek me with
a devout, pure and
simple heart, and
having found Me
never let Me go.

Scivias, Book Three, Vision Ten

GIVING GLORY TO GOD

This is what your Creator does. God loves you
exceedingly, for you are God's creature; and
God gives you the best of treasures, a vivid
intelligence. God commands you through the
words of the law to profit from your intellect
in good works, and grow rich in virtue, that the
Creator, the Good Giver, may thereby be clearly
known. Hence you must think every hour
about how to make so great a gift as useful to
others as to yourself by works of justice, so
that it will reflect the splendour of sanctity
from you, and people will be inspired by your
good example to praise and honour God.

Scivias, Book Three, Vision Ten

WORDS OF ENCOURAGEMENT

ON MODERATION

As the fruit of the earth is harmed by a freak rainstorm, and as from untilled earth sprout no true fruits, but useless weeds, so a person who toils more than her body can bear is rendered useless in her spirit by ill-judged toil and ill-judged abstinence.

Hildegard's letter to Abbess Hazzecha of Krauftal. After 1160

ON PRIDE

So let all the faithful flee from Pride, which always consists in lying, for it cannot be called craftsman either bronze or earthenware. So it builds nothing, either in heavenly or earthly things, but is the destroyer and despoiler of what is built – for it lost heaven and deceived human beings, as Scripture tells.

A letter of advice

ADVICE ON DEALING WITH NIGHTMARES

Servant of God, you who are outstanding in Christ's service, do not fear the oppressiveness that terrifies you in your sleep; it arises in you through your sanguine humours being stirred by a melancholy temperament. That is why your sleep is burdened, and most often the visions in your dreams are not true, because the ancient deceiver, though he does not harm your senses, nonetheless by his deception troubles you in this… Each night, place your hand on your heart, read the Gospel 'In the beginning was the Word' with devout intention, and then say these words:

'Almighty Lord God… free me from this harrowing disquiet, and defend me from all ambushes of airy spirits.'

Letter of advice to a man suffering from nightmares

HUMAN
RESPONSIBILITY

MERCY SPEAKS TO OUR HARDNESS OF HEART

I dwell in the dew and in the air and in all
greenness. My heart fills to overflowing and
I give help to others. I was there when the first
words resounded: 'Let there be'. From these
words the whole of creation issued forth which
stands today at the disposal of humanity. But
you are excluded. With a loving eye, I observe
the demands of life and feel myself a part of all.
I lift up the broken-hearted and lead them to
wholeness, since I am the balm for every pain,
and since my words ring true while you remain
what you are: a bitter cloud of smoke!

Liber vitae meritorum, Part One

GOD WILLS TO PROTECT AND RENEW THE EARTH

As often as the misdeeds of human beings pollute the elements, God will use human torments and calamities to purify them again; for God wants a clean earth, and will not allow it to be harmed or destroyed through human actions.

Liber vitae meritorum, Part Three

HUMAN ·ACTIONS POLLUTE THE EARTH

Noxious fumes hinder the winds on their escapades, so that they are no longer capable of blowing pure air; ominous and threatening thunder rumbles about. As the wind spews filth on account of the numerous misdeeds of human beings, the air emits a poisonous moistness which dries up the greenness and fertility needed to provide nourishment for human life. This layer of cloud is full of snow, from which harmful grubs come into being. They injure and devour the fruits of the earth so that people are unable to derive any benefit from them, because humans beings have closed their hearts and minds to virtue and fail to speak wisdom and truth.

Liber vitae meritorum, Part Three

GOD SHOULD BE THE CENTRE OF OUR LIVES

God created human beings to be full of light so that they could see the radiance of pure ether and hear the songs of the angels. God clothed humanity in such radiance that it shone in splendour. But all of this was lost when human beings disobeyed God's commandment and brought about the fall of nature as well as themselves. Yet the natural elements retained a glimmering of their former pristine state, which human beings could not destroy completely. For this reason people should retain a glimmering of their knowledge of God. They should allow God to return to the centre of their lives, recognizing that they owe their very existence to no one else save God alone, who is the Creator of all.

Liber vitae meritorum, Part Four

THE RICHES OF VIRGINITY

By their purity of purpose, these women have
overcome their vain, empty, unpredictable desires.
Through their passionate love for the true Son,
they have ascended to that level beyond the
confines of prescribed laws and now they breathe
a new air, an air pure beyond the clarity of the
purest water; and they shine with a radiance
beyond the radiant glory of the sun. In the green
life of their virginity and in the blossoming of
body and spirit, these women have revealed their
sweetest longings. Inspired by the Holy Spirit,
they have been filled with the fragrance and
power of many virtues. And now they feel the
breath of a new air, air that breathes the fresh
green force of all the herbs and flowers of earth
and paradise; air that is filled with the fragrance
of life-giving power, just as the summer is filled
with the perfume of green plants and flowers.

Liber vitae meritorum, Part Six

THE TRINITY

PRAISE TO THE TRINITY

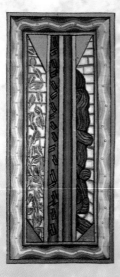

Praise to the Trinity
Who is sound and life,
Creator and sustainer
Of all beings;
The angels praise You,
Who in the splendour
Of your hidden mysteries
Pour out life abundant.

Symphonia armonie celestium revelationum

THE FATHER

The Father is brightness, and that brightness
has brilliance, and that brilliance has fire,
and they are one. Those who do not grasp
this in faith do not see God because they try
to separate God from what he is – for God
is not to be divided... This brightness is the
Father's love. All things are born from it and
it surrounds all things, because they derive
from its power.

From Hildegard's letter to Eberhard II, Bishop of Bamberg, 1163-64

THE SON

The Father arranges, but the Son performs. For the Father has ordained all things in himself, and the Son has carried them out. The light is part of the light which was there in the beginning, before time and eternity, and this is the Son who shines from the Father – the Son through whom all creatures were made. And the Son, who had never before appeared in bodily form, even put on the outer form of man, whom he had fashioned from mud. In this way, God saw all the works before him as light, and when he said 'Let there be', each thing took on an outer form according to its type.

From Hildegard's letter to Eberhard II, Bishop of Bamberg, 1163-64

THE HOLY SPIRIT

In the Holy Spirit there is the union of eternity
and identity. The Holy Spirit is like a fire — but
not an extinguishable fire, at one moment visibly
ablaze, at another, quenched. For the Holy Spirit
produces eternity and identity, and joins them so
that they are one, just as someone binds together
a bundle. For if a bundle were not bound
together, it would not be a bundle but would be
scattered… The Holy Spirit is the fire and life
in that eternity and identity, because God is
alive. For the sun is bright and its light blazes
and it burns that fire that illuminates all the
world; and yet it appears as a single entity.

Anything in which there is no force is dead,
just as the wood torn from the tree is dry because
it has no power of greening. For the Holy Spirit
is the strengthener and the quickener.

From Hildegard's letter to Eberhard II, Bishop of Bamberg, 1163-64

THE HARMONY
OF THE
CELESTIAL SPHERES

SONG TO THE VIRGIN MARY

Hail, O greenest branch
Who came forth with the saints
Like a gust of wind.
When the time came
For your branches to blossom
You were truly exalted,
For the sun's warmth
Perfumed the air around you like
    balsam.
For in you blossomed the fairest flower
From which all dried spices
Derive their perfume.
And your branches
Burst into greenness.
The heavens laid their dew on the grass
And the earth rejoiced,
Because your womb brought forth
    wheat
For the birds of heaven
To make their nests.

Then a banquet was prepared for
    humanity,
And great was our joy.
And in you, O sweet Virgin,
Is there no lack of rejoicing.
Eve hated these things,
But now let us praise the Most High.

Symphonia armonie celestium revelationum

SONG IN HONOUR OF SAINT DISIBOD

O green finger of God
In whom God planted a vineyard
That is resplendent in heaven,
Like a pillar of light.
You are made glorious in your work
    for God.
You are like a high mountain
Which will never be brought low
By God's judgement;
You stand afar off, an exile;
And the armed man
Has not the power to seize you.
Glory be to the Father
And to the Son
And to the Holy Spirit.

Symphonia armonie celestium revelationum

In Praise of Virginity

Green life, most noble,
Rooted in the sun,
Bright and serene,
You shine in a sphere
Beyond all earthly excellence.
You are enfolded
In the embrace of
Divine ministries.
You blush like the dawn,
And like the sun's flame
You burn.

Symphonia armonie celestium revelationum

SONG FOR SAINT URSULA

Blood's crimson
Flowing from a height
Touched by God.
You are a blossom
Which the winter
Of the serpent's breath
Did not harm.

Symphonia armonie celestium revelationum

Text Acknowledgments

I would like to thank the publishers below for permission to reproduce texts from the following editions, and Mark Atherton for his helpful suggestions. Almost all the translations from previous sources have been adapted, in particular to ensure that inclusive language is used throughout. Unless otherwise stated the translations are my own.

Numbers 1, 2, 3, 4 & 8 are adapted from Robert Carver's translations in *Hildegard of Bingen: An Anthology*, edited and introduced by Fiona Bowie and Oliver Davies, SPCK, London, & Crossroad, New York, 1990.

Numbers 5, 6 & 7 are translated from *Hildegard von Bingen, Welt und Mensch. Das Buch "De Operatione Dei"*, translated into modern German from the Gent Codex by Heinrich Schipperges, Otto Müller Verlag, Salzberg, 1965.

Numbers 9, 10, 11, 12, 13 & 14 are based on translations in *Hildegard of Bingen: Scivias*, translated by Mother Columba Hart and Jane Bishop, Classics of Western Spirituality, Paulist Press, New York, 1990.

Numbers 15, 16, 17, 24, 25 & 26 are based on translations by Peter Dronke in *Women Writers of the Middle Ages*, Cambridge University Press, 1988. The letters are from the Berlin Manuscript Lat. Qu. 674.

Numbers 18, 21 & 22 are based on translations by Mark Atherton and Oliver Davies in *Hildegard of Bingen: An Anthology*, edited and introduced by Fiona Bowie and Oliver Davies, SPCK, London, & Crossroad, New York, 1990, in turn based on Hildegard's *Liber vitae meritorum*, in J.P. Pitra's *Analecta sacra*, vol. VIII.

Numbers 19 & 20 are translated from the critical edition of *Hildegardis liber vitae meritorum*, edited by Angela Carlevaris, *Corpus christianorum continuato mediaevalis* XC, Brepols, 1995.

References for 23, 27, 28, 29 & 30 relate to the critical edition, *Saint Hildegard of Bingen, Symphonia*, introduced and translated by Barbara Newman, Cornell University Press, Ithaca and London, 1986. The translations of nos. 29 and 30 are by Oliver Davies and are taken from *Hildegard of Bingen: An Anthology*, edited and introduced by Fiona Bowie and Oliver Davies, SPCK, London, & Crossroad, New York, 1990.

Picture Acknowledgments

All illustrations are reproduced from *Hildegard von Bingen: Wisse die were (Scivias)* with the permission of the publisher, Otto Müller Verlag, Salzburg.